Mel Bay Presents
Piano for Seniors

by Gail Smith

1 2 3 4 5 6 7 8 9 0

© 2009 BY MEL BAY PUBLICATIONS, INC., PACIFIC, MO 63069.
ALL RIGHTS RESERVED. INTERNATIONAL COPYRIGHT SECURED. B.M.I. MADE AND PRINTED IN U.S.A.
No part of this publication may be reproduced in whole or in part, or stored in a retrieval system, or transmitted in any form
or by any means, electronic, mechanical, photocopy, recording, or otherwise, without written permission of the publisher.

Visit us on the Web at www.melbay.com — E-mail us at email@melbay.com

Contents

About the Author 3	Exercise (Echo) 44
Exercise 4	Canon No. 105 45
You Count 5	Canon No. 106 45
Exercise 6	Exercise (Touch Technique) 46
More Beginning Notes 7	Etude in C 47
Exercise 8	Ecossaise 48
Silent Auction 9	It's A Gift to Be Simple 49
Exercise 10	The Ladder of Success 50
Crossword Puzzle 11	We are Climbing Jacob's Ladder 51
Steps 12	Scaling Down 52
Copy Cat 13	America, the Beautiful 53
Exercise 14	Ode to Joy 54
Tie Score 15	Smooth Sailing 55
Exercise 16	When the Saints 56
Two Sides to Everything 17	Blue Mode 57
Mini Waltz 18	Pachelbel's Canon 58
The Spin 19	Dancing 60
The Humming Bird 20	Window Shopping 61
Peaceful March 21	Nocturne Theme 62
Exercise in a new left hand position 22	Evening Melody 63
Mock Rock 23	Enjoy 64
Exercise 24	Theme from Claire de Lune 65
Bach's Musette 25	Late Night Jazz 66
Greta's Gigg 26	Yodel on the Keys 67
Up the Staircase 27	Carousel 68
Prelude in C 28	Keep on Going 69
Two Party Invention 29	Jogging Along 70
Exercise 30	Party Time 71
Welcome Home 31	The Blue Danube Waltz 72
Exercise (Half-Steps) 32	Rage Over a Lost Penny 74
Für Elise 33	Symphony Theme 76
The Can Can 34	Secrets 77
Mozart's Minuet 35	Arabesque 78
The Marine's Hymn 36	I Lost My Keys 80
You're a Grand Old Flag 37	Twelve Bar Blues 81
Exercise 38	I Got the Blues 82
Hannah 39	Feeling Good 83
Exercise (Skip A Note - Hanon Etude) 40	Star Dust 84
Spring 41	Theme and Variation 86
Ancient Bagpipes 43	

About the Author

Gail Smith was born in Bridgeport, Connecticut, on January 26. Gail's father, Carl Erick Johnson, sang tenor in the church choir. Her mother, Ethel, played the piano and had Gail start piano lessons.

Smith received her Bachelor of Fine Arts Degree from Florida Atlantic University. She has taught piano students from the age of 3 to 96! Her blind student, Ivan, was seen on national TV. Giving musical lecture recitals by portraying the composer's wife has been an effective way to reach audiences with the history of music. Gail has portrayed Marian MacDowell and Anna Magdalena Bach. She gives many workshops and concerts throughout the United States as well as in Germany, Sweden and Japan.

Smith's life has revolved around her family, church and music. She has been active in many organizations including being national Music Chairman of the National League of American Pen Women and is a former president of the Broward County branch. Ms. Smith is also a member of The Freedoms Foundation of Valley Forge, National Music Teachers Association, and Federation of Music Clubs.

Ms. Smith's works include many piano solos, choral works, a piano trio, a composition for four pianos and numerous vocal solos. She has arranged hundreds of hymns, Indian melodies, and folk tunes from many countries. Her trademark is her piano palindromes, which can be played backwards as well as forwards and sound the same.

She is the author of: Complete Church Pianist, Sunday Morning Pianist, Four Centuries of Women Composers, Celebrate the Piano Series, Hymns Made Easy, Piano Chords Made Easy, Complete Book of Modulations for the Pianist, Complete Book of Exercises for the Pianist, and Complete Improvisation, Fills & Chord Progressions Book.

Gail also composed the world's first reversible piano solo, which sounds the same upside down and is titled "WOW MOM". She loves researching the history of music and wishes to pass on her enthusiasm for piano study to all ages of beginning students, especially seniors.

Exercise

Alternate between the Right and Left Hands.

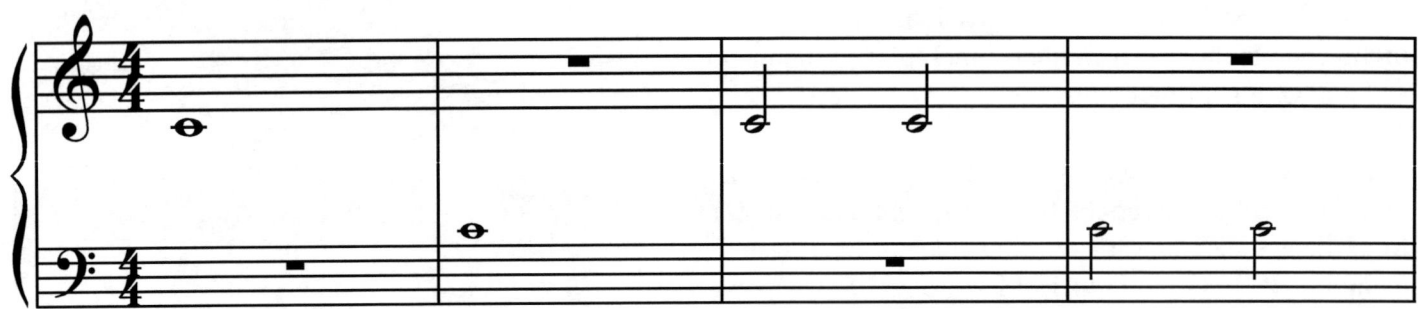

Theory Question

What kinds of notes are there?

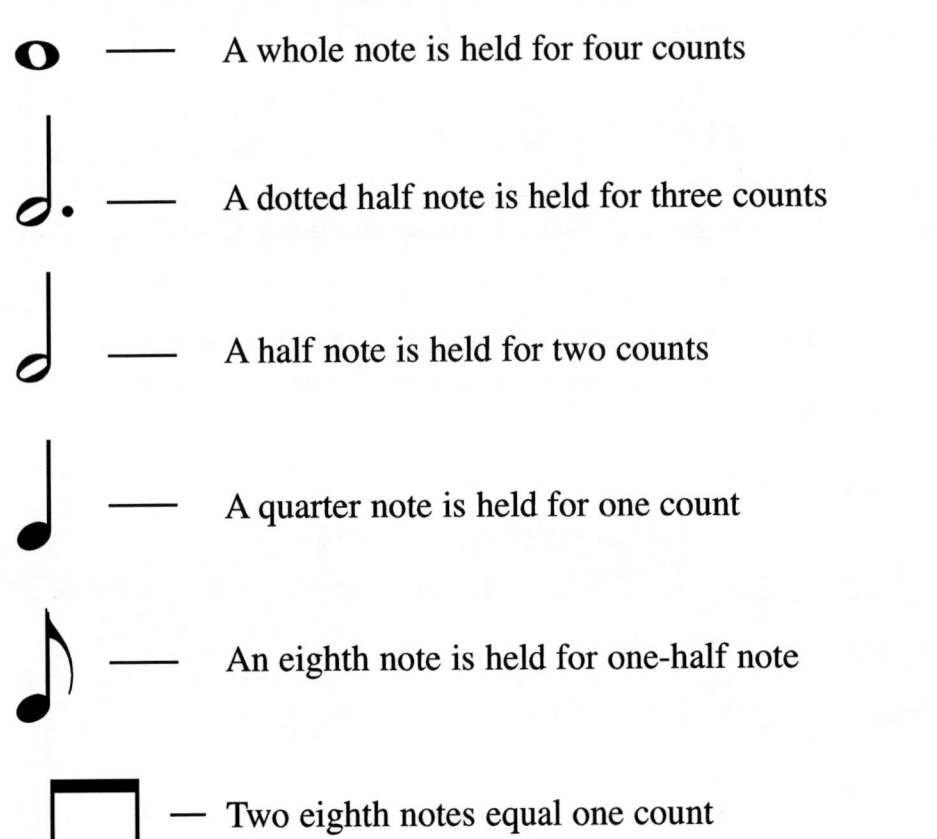

- A whole note is held for four counts
- A dotted half note is held for three counts
- A half note is held for two counts
- A quarter note is held for one count
- An eighth note is held for one-half note
- Two eighth notes equal one count

You Count

Gail Smith

Exercise

Each finger plays a note, one hand at a time.

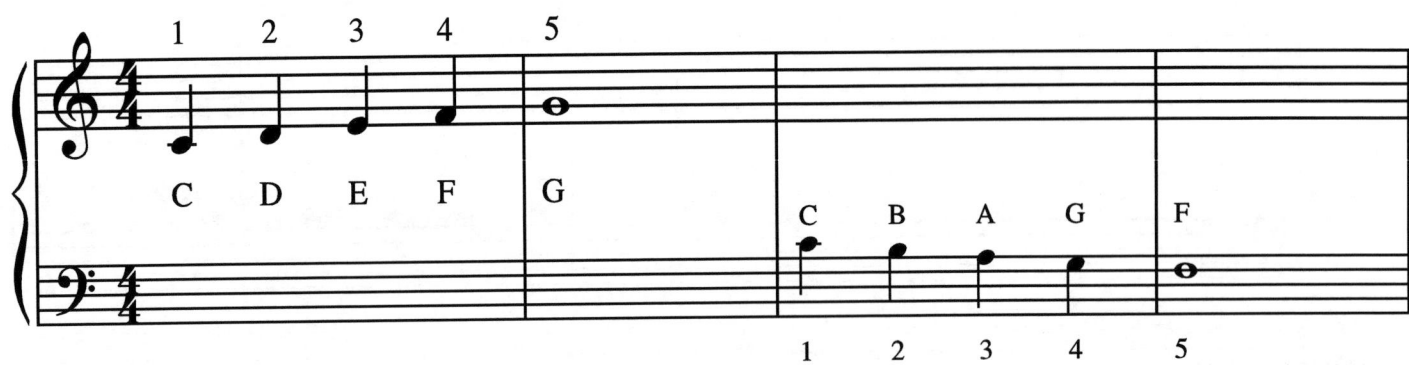

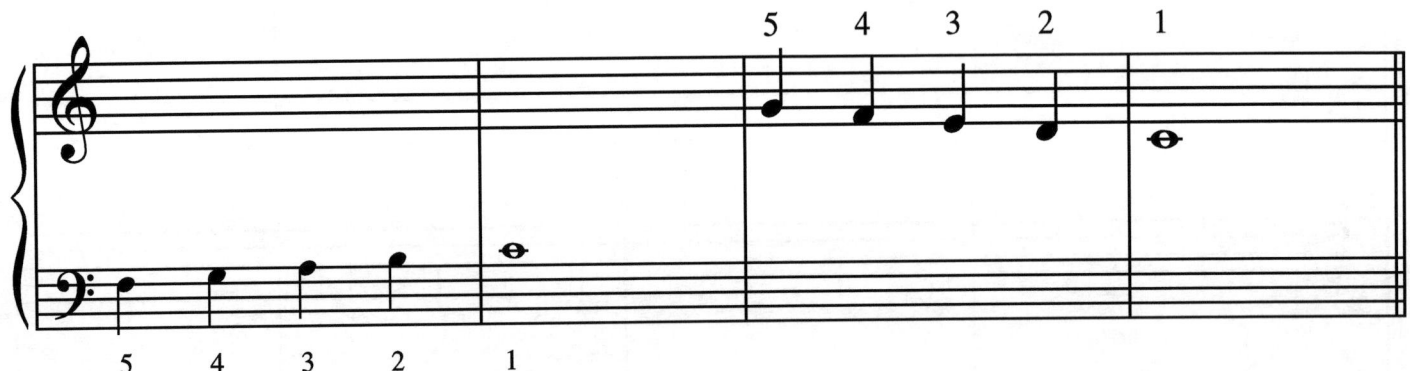

Theory Question

What are the names of the notes on the lines and spaces?

In the Treble Clef they are:

In the Bass Clef they are:

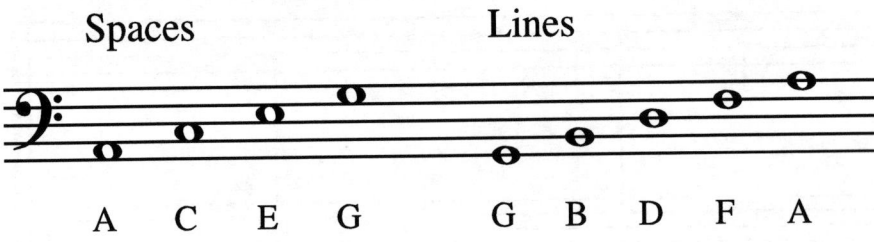

More Beginning Notes

Dedicated to Alexandra Katherine Grace Rodriguez

Gail Smith

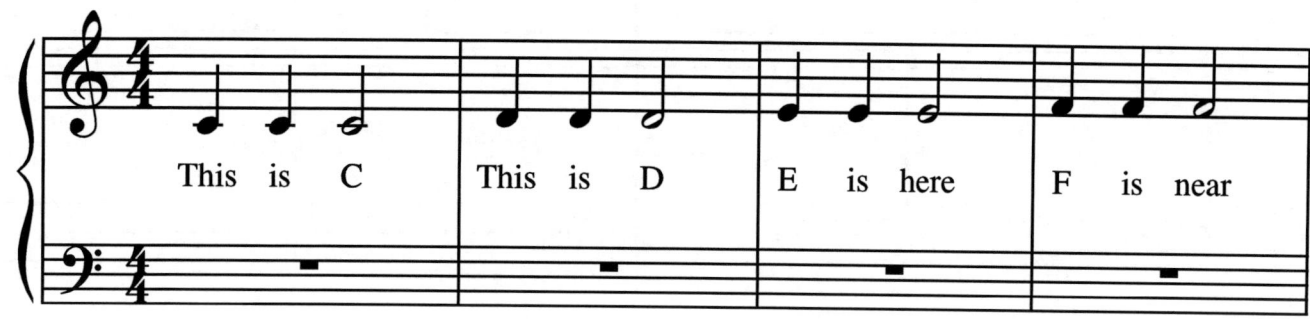
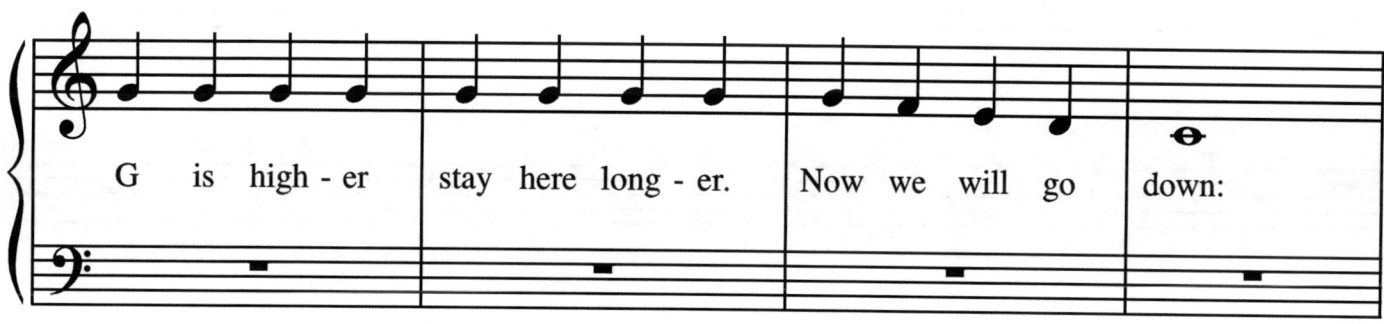

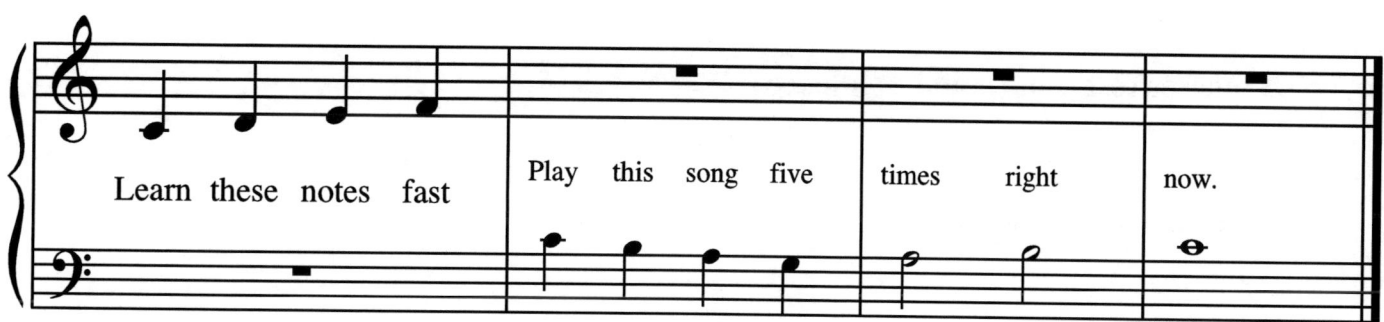

Exercise

Counting rests and playing the note C

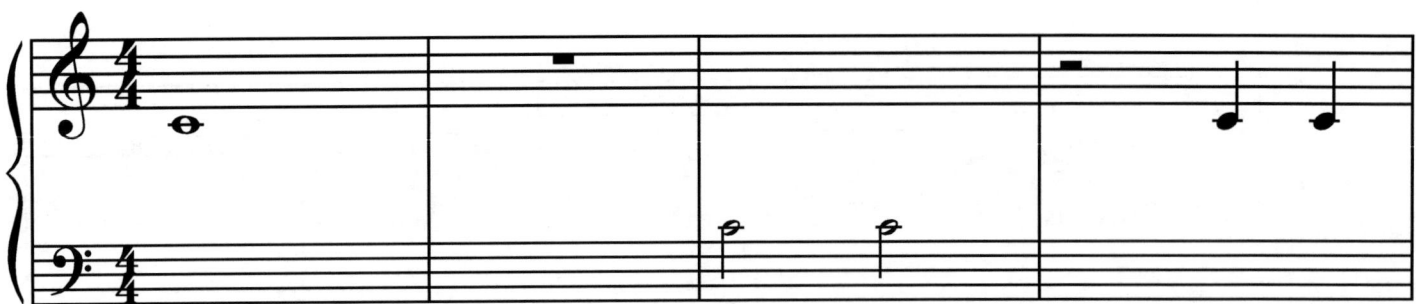

Theory Question

What are rest signs?

A rest is a unit of silence.

▬ — A whole rest - four counts of silence

▬ — A half rest - two counts of silence

𝄽 — A quarter rest - one count of silence

𝄾 — An eighth rest - one-half count of silence

Silent Auction

Exercise

Theory Question

What are musical dynamic marks?

ff —— play very loud

f —— play loud

mf —— play medium loud

mp —— play medium soft

p —— play soft

pp —— play very soft

forte —— loud

piano —— soft

crescendo —— gradually play louder

decrescendo —— gradually play softer

Crossword Puzzle

Gail Smith

Steps
(2 note phrases)

Gail Smith

Copy Cat

Gail Smith

Exercise

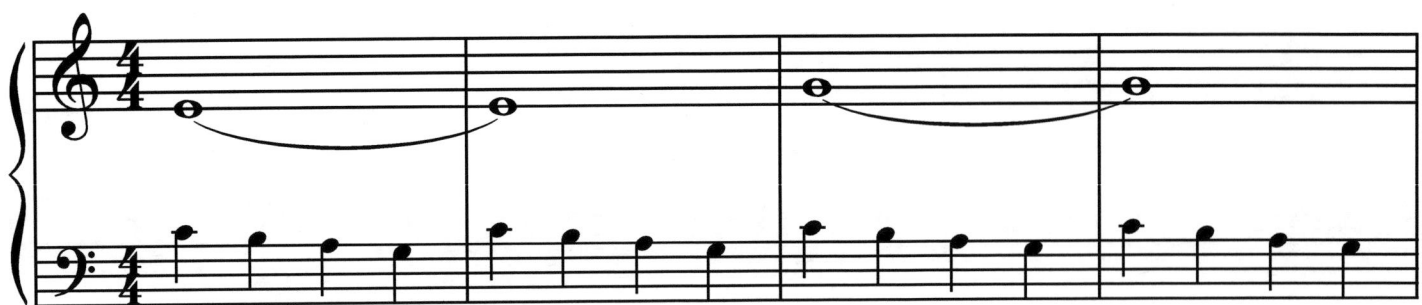

Theory Question

What is a musical tie?

A curved line connecting two or more continuous notes which are the same pitch. Hold the note for the full value of both notes. In the example above, you would hold the note for eight counts.

Tie Score

Dedicated to Marla and Marissa

Gail Smith

Exercise

Finger Dexterity in holding a finger down.

Theory Question

What are bar lines?

Bar lines divide the song into measures, in this exercise there are four counts to each measure. There are eight measures in this exercise.

A double bar line is always put at the end of a song.

Two Sides to Everything

Gail Smith

Mini Waltz

Gail Smith

Theory Question

What is a waltz?

A waltz is a song or dance with three counts to a measure. The dance has three steps.

The Spin

Gail Smith

Allegro

The Humming Bird

Gail Smith

Peaceful March

Gail Smith

Exercises in a new left-hand position

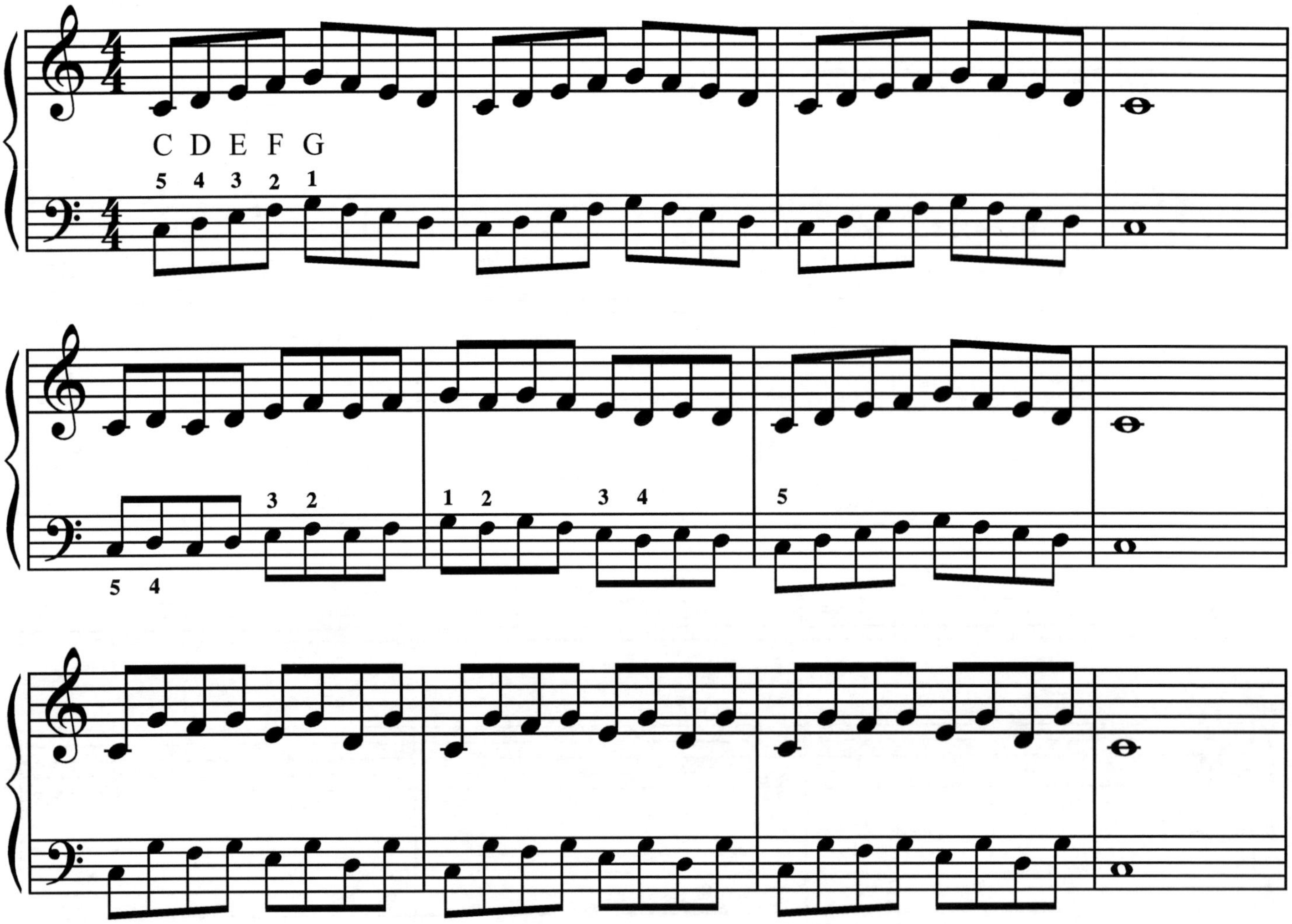
C D E F G
5 4 3 2 1
3 2
1 2
3 4
5
5 4

Theory Question

What is an interval?

It is the distance between two notes such as:

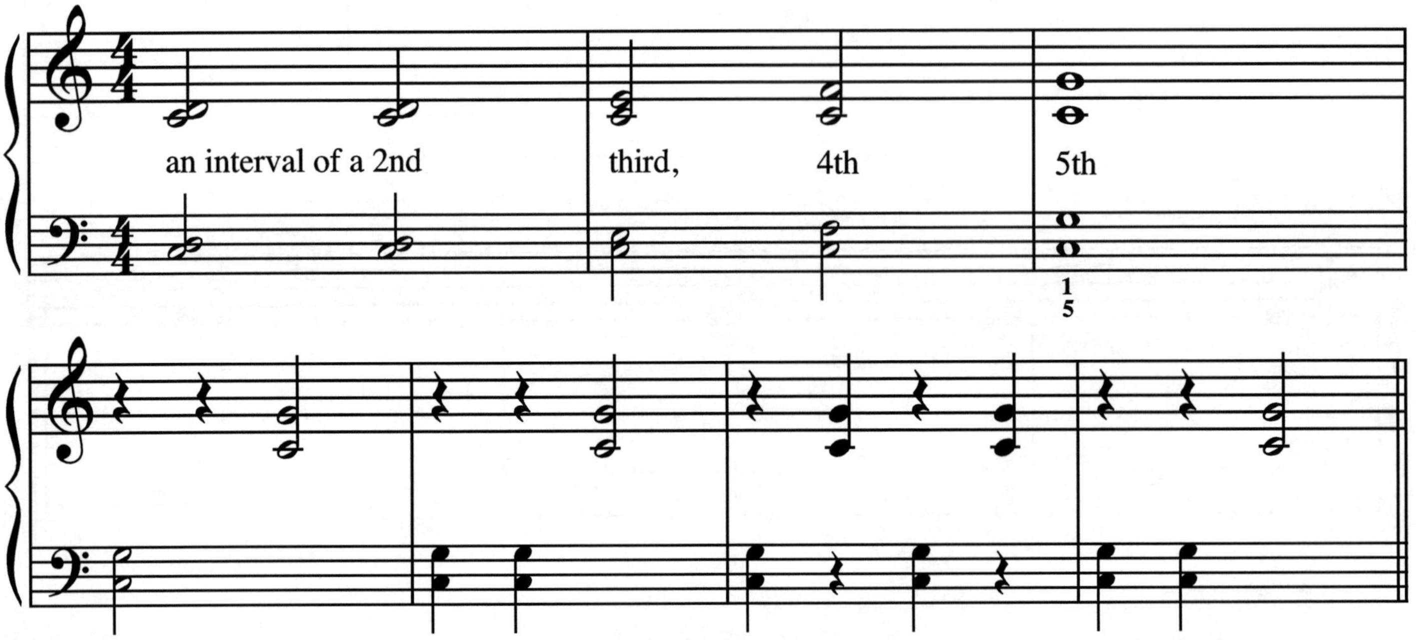
an interval of a 2nd
third,
4th
5th
1
5

Mock Rock

Gail Smith

Exercise

Theory Question

What is a time signature?

At the beginning of each song there are numbers such as 4/4 3/4 2/4

4/4 Time — The top number means a quarter note gets one count. The bottom number means a quarter note gets one count.

3/4 Time — The top number means there are three counts to each measure. The bottom number means a quarter note gets one count.

2/4 Time — The top number means there are two counts in each measure.

6/8 Time — The top number means there are six counts in each measure. The bottom number means an eighth note gets one count.

Bach's Musette

Arranged by Gail Smith

Greta's Gigg

Dedicated to Greta Worden

Gail Smith

Up the Staircase

Gail Smith

Prelude in C

Gail Smith

Two Party Invention

Gail Smith

Exercise

Theory Question

What do these tempo markings mean?

Presto — very, very fast

Allegro — fast

Moderato — medium tempo

Andante — a walking tempo

Lento — a slow tempo

Largo — play very slow

Welcome Home

Gail Smith

Exercise (Half-Steps)

Theory Question

What are accidentals?

They are:

Flats ♭   A flat lowers a note one half-step.

Double flat ♭♭   A double flat lowers a note a whole step.

Sharp ♯   A sharp raises a note a half-step.

Double sharp 𝄪   A double sharp raises a note a whole step.

Natural ♮   A natural cancels a sharp or flat that has previously been sharped or played as a flat.

Fermata 𝄐   Hold the note under the fermata.

Für Elise

Beethoven
Arranged by Gail Smith

Moderato

33

The Can Can

Gail Smith

Mozart's Minuet

Arranged by Gail Smith

The Marines' Hymn

You're a Grand Old Flag

Dedicated to Daniel Rodriguez

Exercise

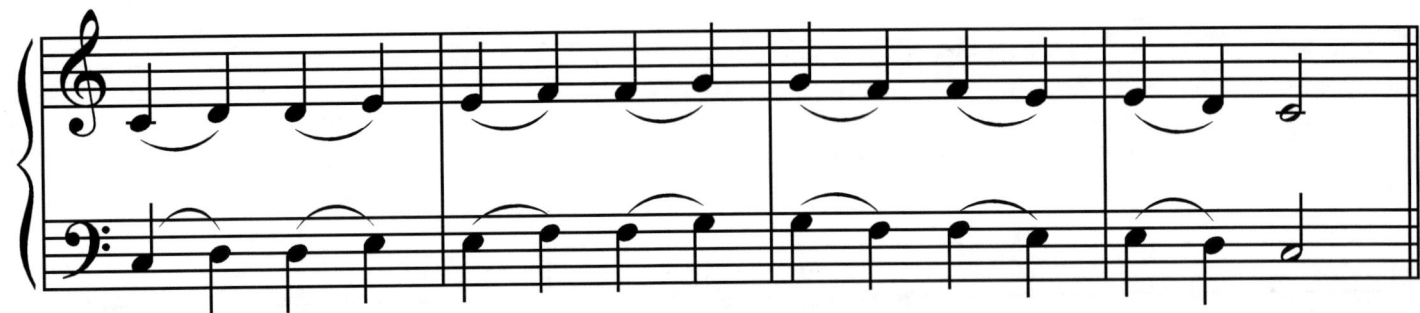

Theory Questions

What is a musical palindrome?

It is a song that sounds the same whether it is played backwards or forward.

Palindrome words are: radar, level, mom, dad.

A palindrome sentence is: Sit on a potato pan Otis.

What is a Semordnilap?

A word that has meaning backwards and forward.

Stressed is desserts backwards and is called a semordnilap. Another example is warts and straw.

Words are interesting and palindromes are great exercises for your eyes, brain and fingers. I hope you enjoy playing the song Hannah both forwards and backwards!

Hannah

(A Palindrome)

Gail Smith

Exercise (Skip A Note - Hanon Etude)

Theory Question

What are sixteenth notes?

1 - ah - & da   2   3   4

It takes four sixteenth notes to equal one count or beat. These notes are played fast.

Spring

Vivaldi
Arranged by Gail Smith

Andante

This page has been left blank to avoid awkward page turns.

Ancient Bagpipes

Gail Smith

Exercise (Echo)

This is an echo or round. The left hand repeats what the right hand just played.

Gail Smith

Theory Question

What is a musical canon?

It is a song that has the same melody starting over usually two measures later that continues as harmony or a second part.

Canon No. 105

Kunz

Canon No. 106

Kunz

Exercise (Touch Technique)

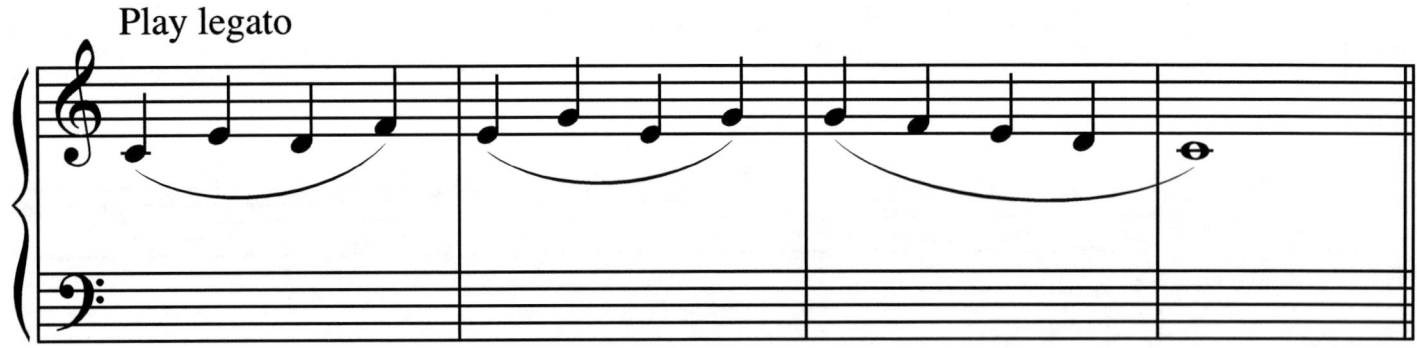

Theory Question

What do these musical terms mean?

Staccato — A dot placed over a note or under. Play the notes detached as if you touched a hot iron.

Legato — Play the notes smooth, connecting one to the next.

Crescendo — Gradually playing louder by pressing harder on the keys with your fingertips.

Decrescendo — Gradually playing softer by pressing the keys lighter.

Etude in C

Op. 108, No. 13

Ludvig Schytte

Allegro moderato ($\dotted{d} = 69$)

Ecossaise

Beethoven
Arranged by Gail Smith

Theory Question

What does L.H. mean?

L.H. stands for the left hand. In this song the left hand crosses over the right hand and plays the high C in the treble clef.

It's A Gift to Be Simple

Folk Song

Arranged by Gail Smith

The Ladder of Success

Gail Smith

Theory Question

What is a scale?

A ladder of sound. There are seven consecutive ascending notes in a scale.

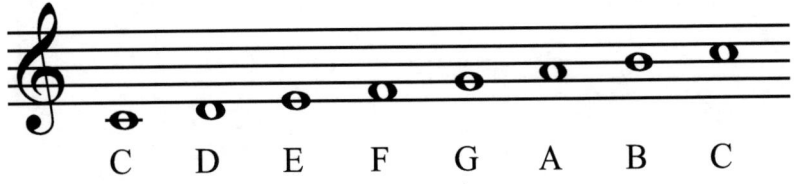

Scaling Down

Moderato

Gail Smith

America, the Beautiful

Katherine Bates *Arranged by Gail Smith*

Ode to Joy

Beethoven
Arranged by Gail Smith

Smooth Sailing

Gail Smith

Moderato

When the Saints

Spiritual

Arranged by Gail Smith

*A Triad

Theory Question

What is a triad?

A triad is three notes played together forming a chord.

Blue Mode

Gail Smith

D.C. al Fine
This means to go back to the beginning of the song and play it till *Fine*.

Pachelbel's Canon

Arranged by Gail Smith

Variation II

Variation III

Variation IV

Dancing

Gail Smith

Window Shopping

Gail Smith

Nocturne Theme

Chopin

Arranged by Gail Smith

Theory Question

What is a turn signal?

A turn was used in romantic music to embellish a note by turning around the note completely.

Playing the note then going above, back and below the note.

Evening Melody

Gail Smith

Enjoy

Jazzy Gail Smith

Theme from Claire de Lune

Claude Debussy
Arranged by Gail Smith

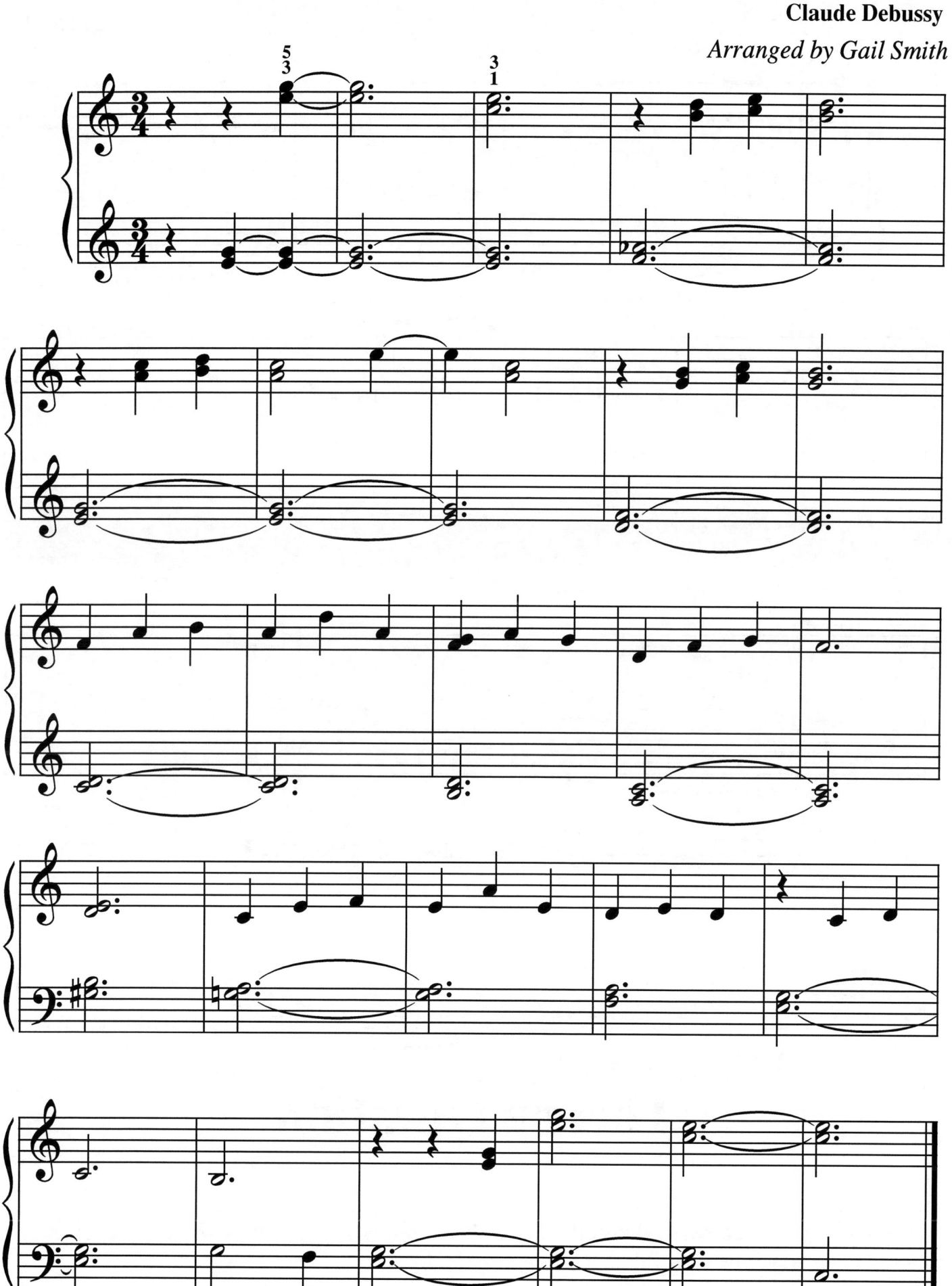

Late Night Jazz

Gail Smith

Theory Question

What is a ledger line?

When notes are placed below the staff we call the extra lines ledger lines. We use ledger lines to write notes lower or higher than the five line staff.

Yodel on the Keys

Dedicated to Alex Hall

Gail Smith

Carousel

Gail Smith

Keep on Going

Gail Smith

Jogging Along

Gail Smith

Party Time

Gail Smith

The Blue Danube Waltz

Johann Strauss
Arranged by Gail Smith

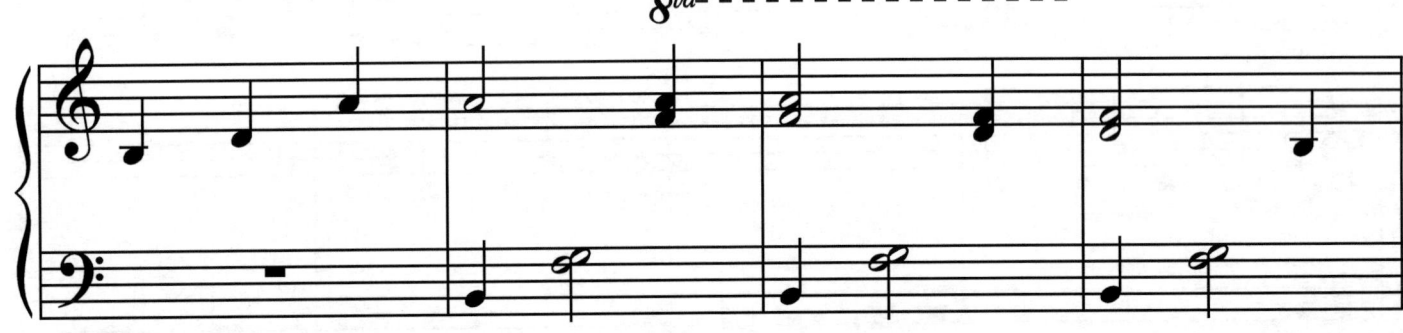

Theory Question

What does 8va mean?

Play the notes an octave (8 notes) higher.

Rage Over a Lost Penny

Beethoven
Arranged by Gail Smith

Symphony Theme

Mozart
Arranged by Gail Smith

Secrets

Gail Smith

Johann Friedrich Burgmüller
(1806 - February 13, 1874)

Johann Friedrich Burgmüller was a great German pianist and composer who wrote numerous piano works.

Arabesque

Johann Friedrich Burgmüller

I Lost My Keys

Dedicated to Lon

Gail Smith

Twelve Bar Blues

Gail Smith

I Got the Blues

Gail Smith

Feeling Good

Gail Smith

Star Dust

H. Carmichael

Arranged by Gail Smith

Theme and Variation

Gurlitt Op. 228

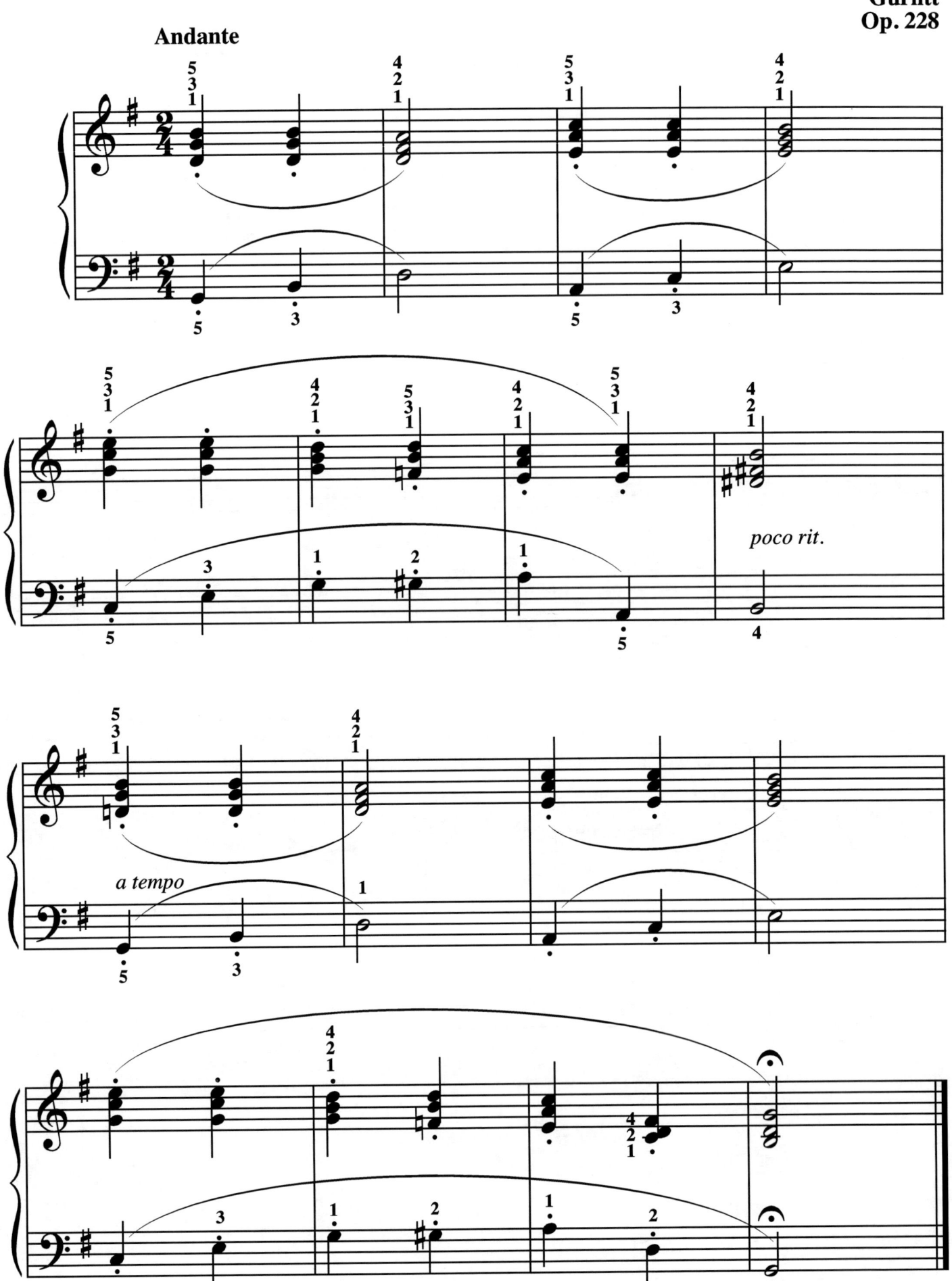

Moderato

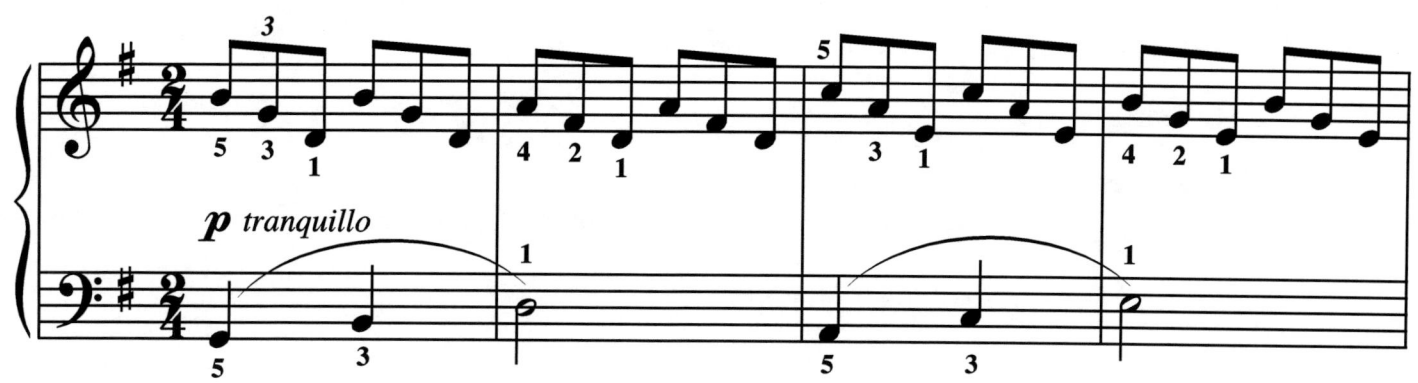

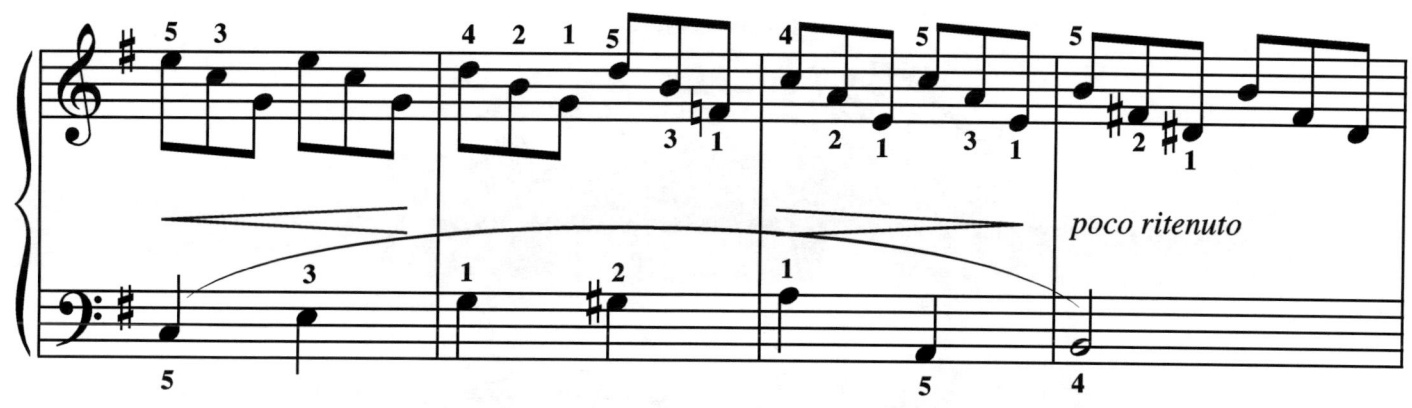

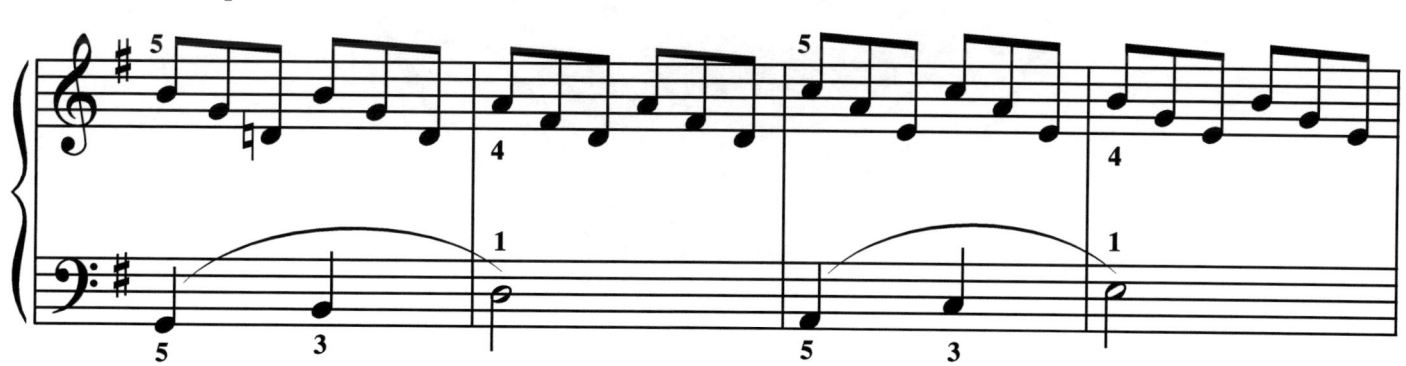

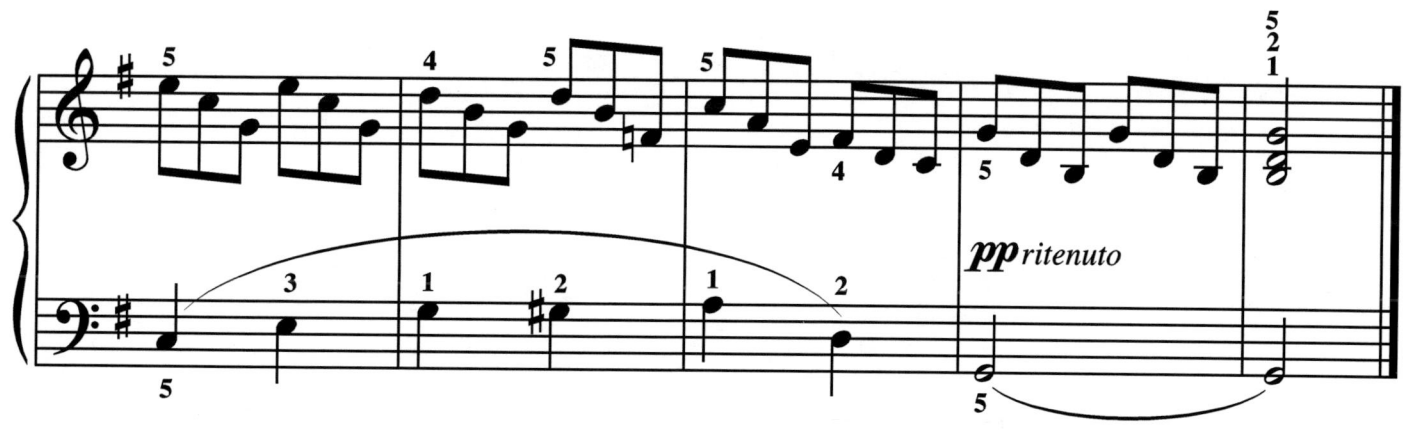